Kid Concoctions

by Robynne Eagan

illustrated by Darcy Tom

Teaching & Learning Company

1204 Buchanan St., P.O. Box 10
Carthage, IL 62321

The activities demonstrated on the front cover are
Purple Volcano (page 22), Slime (page 30) and Creepy Clay (page 34).

Cover by Girard Photography

Copyright © 1994, Teaching & Learning Company

ISBN No. 1-57310-008-0

Printing No. 987654321

Teaching & Learning Company
1204 Buchanan St., P.O. Box 10
Carthage, IL 62321

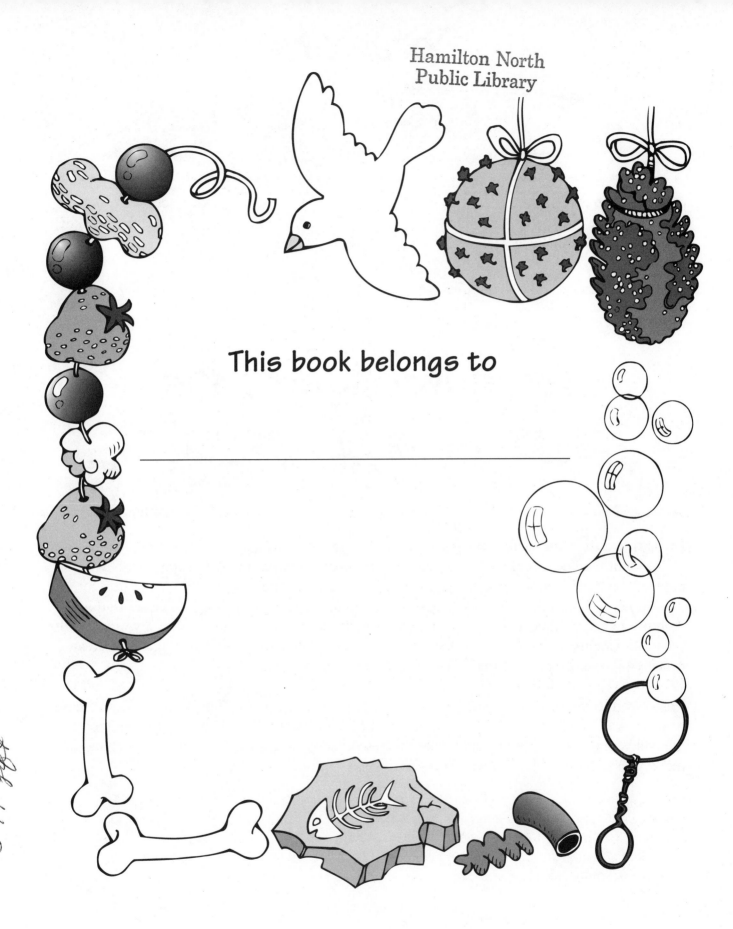

This book belongs to

_____

Foreword

This resource is full of weird and wonderful kid-appealing concoctions for neat stuff to make and do. These concoctions tap into kids' curiosity and natural learning style to enhance skill development and make any curriculum topic more interesting.

Acknowledgements

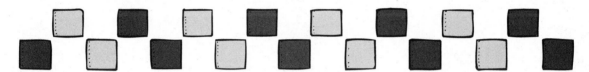

I would like to acknowledge my grandfather "Bertie" Johnson's contribution to this collection. He brought me buckets of sand and pumped basins of water for my first experiments with the physical properties of materials. To Rusty Cochrane and Dennise Matson, recognition for making those first mud pies with me, for pouring and stirring everything we could find in the bathroom sink and for your continued creative suggestions. And thank you to my grandmothers Edith Cochrane and Elizabeth Johnson for allowing us to crack our own eggs and create messes as we experimented and made discoveries over the years.

Thank you to the educators, parents and children who have offered suggestions and who have in some way helped to create the concoctions in this collection. And special appreciation to the educators who taught me and those I have worked with, for helping me to understand that the key to teaching is to excite a child's curiosity.

Table of Contents

Dear Teacher or Parent,

Unleash the mad scientists lurking within your students! Mix kids, nature and a simple kitchen laboratory to turn your classroom into a bubbling, brewing learning environment with *Kid Concoctions*—a lively collection of extraordinary things that kids can make and do using ordinary ingredients.

Would your students enjoy stirring up some goop, slime or fizz? Or brewing some bubbles—tiny ones that won't stop growing or huge ones that will amaze? Would they like to try a formula that gives chills on a dark night? Would they like to snack on spooky candy that sparks in the dark, eat a flower or a rubber egg? Are they looking for a formula that will help make friends with some wild critters? Formulas for fizzing potions, bubbles, crystals, haunting creations, critter food, musical vegetables and fun fill the pages of this resource of fantastic formulas and projects.

The formulas are presented in an easy-to-follow format with symbols for at-a-glance information. Helpful tips and educational follow-up ideas are presented for each activity. These projects are designed to offer creative learning experiences that facilitate skill development and integrate into the curriculum making any topic more interesting.

If you are looking for amazing, delightful, kid-appealing, *educational* fun, then this book is for you.

Sincerely,

Robynne

Robynne Eagan

Symbol Key

These symbols will provide at-a-glance information regarding the preparation of the mixtures.

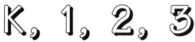 **K, 1, 2, 3**   Recommended grade level

 Full child participation in preparation

 Ingredients may be hard to find

 Partial child participation in preparation

 Gift

 Caution, extra supervision advised

 Large space requirements

 Ten minutes of active preparation time

 Mixture needs cooking

 Ten to sixty minutes of active preparation time

 Material will last for one to two weeks

 Over one hour of active preparation time

 Material will last for one to two months

 Good group project

 Material will last for over three months

 Edible

 Messy

Measurement Equivalents

These will be useful if you divide recipes into small units to enable greater participation.

1 tablespoon = 3 teaspoons
$1/2$ tablespoon = $1^1/2$ teaspoons
4 tablespoons = $1/4$ cup
5 tablespoons and 1 teaspoon = $1/3$ cup

Metric Conversions:

1 dry ounce = 28 grams
1 dry pound = 373 grams
1 liquid ounce = 29.5 milliliters
1 cup = .24 liter
1 pint = .47 liter
1 quart = .95 liter
1 gallon = 3.8 liters

1 cup = 250 milliliters
$1/2$ cup = 125 milliliters
1 teaspoon = 5 milliliters
1 tablespoon = 15 milliliters
$1/4$ cup = 60 milliliters
1 inch = 2.54 centimeters
$1/4$-inch thickness = 5 millimeters thickness

Oven Temperatures:

230°F = 110°C
275°F = 135°C
325°F = 163°C
350°F = 177°C
375°F = 191°C
400°F = 204°C

Guidelines to Facilitate Creative Learning

1. Respect a child's right to explore. Provide materials, resources and stimulating ideas that will lead children to their own questions and discoveries.

2. Introduce skills, techniques and information in response to a child's curiosity and needs.

3. Organize. Have clear aims and objectives in mind. Read instructions, have materials ready and go through a trial run. Children should be able to experiment and make discoveries with little assistance.

4. Be flexible. Students may not make the discoveries you expect.

5. Learn to recognize and praise children's skills of problem solving, questioning, observation, analysis and discovery.

6. Promote children's confidence in their own abilities.

7. Evaluate the child's progress through observation of many experiences. Offer positive comments on the processes mastered and the concepts grasped.

8. Prepare for some degree of mess. Encourage students to participate in the planning and cleaning of a creative learning environment suitable to everyone involved.

Chapter 1

Kid Crafts
Rainbow Potion

K-3

Materials:

jar
1 ounce (29.57 ml) cup
small fork
1 T (15 ml) cooking oil
4 drops each of red, blue and green food coloring
water

Process:

1. Fill the jar with water.

2. Pour cooking oil into the cup.

3. Add 4 drops of each of the food coloring colors.

4. Beat the oil and colors with a fork until thoroughly mixed.

5. Pour the mixture of oil and food coloring onto the water.

6. Keep the jar still and observe for 5 to 10 minutes.

Try This:

- Set this up as a center. Allow children to explore with the oil, water and colors.
- What happens when this mixture is stirred up?
- Encourage students to observe and discuss what they see.
- Small pools of oil spotted with tiny spheres of color float on the surface of the water. Individual spheres of color appear to explode outward, producing flat circles of color on the surface of the water with streams of color that sink down through the water. Food coloring is water-based, and oil and water do not mix.

Mud Pie

K-3

A favorite old classic.

Materials:

sand
clean dirt
water (as needed)
cake pan or pie plate

tiny stones, sand, leaves, grass,
    wildflowers, seeds
sunshine
large bowl or pail

Process:

1. Mix clean sand, dirt and some water with your hands in the large bowl or pail.

2. Add more water as needed, but keep the mixture really thick.

3. Line a cake pan or pie plate with grass to prevent sticking.

4. Pour the mixture into the pan.

5. Sprinkle on a layer of tiny stones; dry, white sand; or plant material.

6. Add another layer of mud.

7. Decorate with flower petals, leaves, seeds or black mud "icing."

8. Bake in the sun until ready "to serve"!

Try This:

- Have a "bake off" and allow all students to be "judges" choosing the best pie. (You may want to establish several categories so there will be many winners.)
- Encourage creative decorating techniques for this outdoor art class.
- Incorporate with a math activity. Make play money and have students buy and sell pies at the bake shop.
- Have students follow up with a written recipe or a story about the pie.
- Speed the "cooking" process up by putting in a warm oven 150°F (65°C) until the pie starts to crack slightly on the surface. The cooking time will vary according to the size and moisture content of the pie.

Musical Vegetables

2-3   🕑 10-60 min. ⚠ Caution

Materials:

gourd or squash
pointy object (hammer and nail)*

Process:

1. Make some holes into a gourd or squash using a hammer and nail.

2. Leave the gourd or squash to dry for one month.

3. Turn the holey gourd or squash every other day.

4. In one month shake it up, and you will have a maraca.

Try This:

- Have every student make a maraca. Use this as a steppingstone to a class band. Other instruments can be made to complement the maraca band.
- Incorporate the turning of the maracas into the class calendar. Students can use their pattern skills to recognize what days the maracas need to be turned. (Try to start this activity at the beginning of a month.)
- If students have a building center, allow them to use the hammer and nail–punch the holes ahead of time for the sake of saftey.
- Integrate this activity with a harvest unit.

* Caution: Be careful using hammer and nail.

Wishing Dust

K-3

A wonderful way to finish off a school barbecue or campfire.

Materials:

campfire (or charcoal barbecue)
sugar
glitter (optional)
a wish

Process:

1. At the end of a barbecue or campfire sing-along, have children think of a wish.

2. Distribute handfuls (about 1 ounce each) of wishing dust.

3. Children whisper their wish into the dust and keep their hands closed.

4. With adult supervision, each child throws his handful of wishing dust and wish into the fire. The fire will flare brightly and sometimes with color to demonstrate that "the wish was received."

Try This:

- Depending upon the time of year, this may be a special holiday wish, a wish for the summer holiday or a wish for the new school year.

4

Pasta Colors

K-2

macaroni

Materials:

large clear plastic bag
3 drops of food coloring
2 T (30 ml) water
1 package of pasta
tray

Process:

1. Pour uncooked pasta shapes into bag.

2. Add food coloring and water.

3. Shake until the pasta appears well colored.

4. Spread pasta on tray to air dry.

5. When dry, use or store in sealed container for later use.

Try This:

- There are many interesting pasta shapes on the market and various food colors available, allowing for many variations.
- Use as a manipulative for hands-on math programs–it is perfect for sorting and classifying activities. Section off a paper plate and sort away!
- Use for various art and craft activities. Try a pasta collage, a pasta rainbow, a mosaic, thread pasta on a string for jewelry and make a pasta dinner glued to the plate.
- Pasta alphabets can be used for colorful greetings and messages.
- Kids love learning the interesting pasta names. Use these names and record them on a chart for a lesson in letter sounds.

Pasta Creatures

 K-3

Materials:

1 cup (250 ml) of tiny pasta pieces per child (pasta letters or pastina works well)
3 T (45 ml) or more of water for each cup of pasta
food coloring (optional)
large pot or bowl
wooden spoon

Process:

1. Pour the desired amount of pasta into a large pot or bowl.

2. Add food coloring to water if color is desired.

3. Add the water, a little at a time, and stir until the pasta has a sticky, clay-like consistency.

4. Form the pasta mixture into sculptures.

5. Let the sculptures dry thoroughly until they are hard.

Try This:

- Bend a paper clip into a hanging hook. Gently poke one end of the paper clip into the top of the wet sculpture. When it dries, the sculpture can be hung in a place of honor.
- When the sculpture has thoroughly dried, it can be painted.
- Make a sculpture of a snowy village using this material–add some glitter and white paint.

6

Pouring Plastic

2-3

Materials:

1 envelope unflavored gelatin
3 T (45 ml) water
3 drops food coloring
cookie cutters or molds

saucepan
spoon
stove

Process:

1. Add gelatin and water to pot.

2. Add enough food coloring to give you the shade you desire.

3. Cook over medium heat, stirring constantly until everything dissolves and blends together.

4. Pour the mixture into metal cookie cutters or molds.

5. Let dry until the edges are hard and sharp–about 24 hours.

6. When the creations are dry, remove them from their molds.

Try This:

- Pour a thin layer of plastic onto a cookie sheet. Students can cut shapes from this or use a paper punch to punch lots of plastic sequins for later creations.
- Punch holes in creations to thread string through for hanging.
- For broaches and buttons, put pins on the wet plastic to harden.

Water Sculptures

K-3   SPACE

Materials:

water
interesting containers: molds, milk cartons, tin cans, plastic jugs and cups
food coloring
cold weather (below 32°F [0°C])

Process:

1. Round up some interesting containers. Use old cake pans, jelly molds, plastic containers and tin cans. Cardboard milk cartons are perfect for making building blocks.

2. If you want colored blocks, add food coloring to the water.

3. Pour water into the containers and freeze outside until completely hard.

4. Pop the ice blocks out of their containers as they freeze and make more.

5. Place the shapes in the shade so they will last longer.

6. Build, create, carve and paint your ice structures.

Try This:

- Involve the entire class in the planning and building of the ultimate ice fort or more ambitious ice castle. Have students draw up plans, assign tasks and collect containers.
- Sculptures can be created by chipping and carving with blunt tools or by melting and warming with your hands.
- Incorporate this activity into a unit on winter.
- Include this activity in a school winter carnival.

8

Mud Fossils

1-3

Materials:

soil
water
cookie sheet
bowl

spoon
small items: shells, leaves, wood,
　　　　　pebbles, coins, keys

Process:

1. Fill a container half full with soil. Soil with clay in it will work best. Squeeze the soil in your hand–if it adheres together well and forms a ball, it will work.

2. Mix water with soil until the mixture is thick and hand-moldable.

3. Stir in little items such as shells, pebbles, coins, keys or other washable items.

4. Completely conceal the items in the mud.

5. Allow mud to dry for at least 24 hours.

6. Break the mud open with your hands and remove the hidden objects.

7. Now look for the homemade fossils.

Try This:

- Integrate this activity into a study of fossils. After this activity, students will better understand how fossils were formed and what they are.
- Integrate this activity with a unit on dinosaurs.
- Do rubbings of the fossil.
- Make a plaster casting of a fossil by pouring plaster into the impression and letting it dry.
- Take students on a fossil hunt or to a museum to study fossils.
- Treat the activity as an art activity–put a lot of time into planning the layout of the fossil.
- Variation: Use plaster of Paris in place of the mud.

Magic Copper Cleaner

K-3

- -

Materials:
1 cup (250 ml) white vinegar
1/4 cup (60 ml) table salt
bowl
spoon
copper pennies, buttons, cups, jewelry or other items

- -

Process:

1. Pour vinegar into the bowl.

2. Add salt and stir until the solution is clear.

3. Add tarnished items to the bowl and stir gently. The copper pieces will change before your eyes!

- -

Try This:

- Throw hundreds of pennies into the school yard and have children go on a treasure hunt. Stir the pennies into the magic solution and watch in awe. Follow up with math activities using the bright, shiny coppers.

10

Help Save the Earth Concoctions

K-3

Environment friendly, practical concoctions kids can feel good about.

Materials: clean containers with sealing lids
labels
funnels for pouring
See options below.

Wonder Cleaner

Materials:

white distilled vinegar

Process:

1. Pour vinegar into container (a squirt bottle of some sort would be best for this cleaner).

2. Affix label that reads:
   Wonder Cleaner works wonders removing stains, mold, grease and odors. It adds sparkle and shine to windows, mirrors, all glass, paintbrushes and floors. It can add softness to your wash if added in the rinse cycle.

Pure Clean

K-3

Materials: pure soap (can be purchased in grocery or hardware stores in flakes, powder, bars or liquid form)
containers
labels

Process:

1. Put soap into appropriate container for the soap form you are using.

2. Affix a label that reads:
   Keep the environment clean while you clean with Pure Clean. Clean up those clothes, dishes, floors, toys or even your car.

Clean Air

K-3

• •

Materials:
white distilled vinegar
containers with lids
labels

• •

Process:

1. Decorate a container with a tight-sealing lid.

2. Fill the container with vinegar.

3. Add a label that reads:
   Clean Air will absorb odors you don't want around. Remove the lid and let Clean Air start working for your air. Pour into a fancy bowl for a special occasion or place on your stove to warm Clean Air and make it work even harder.

• •

Try This:

- Turn your classroom into a manufacturing plant. Provide students with the information and materials they need to develop product names, design logos, create slogans and package their products. Incorporate this project with a study of manufacturing, advertising and marketing. Help kids to recognize marketing schemes aimed at them.
- Encourage students to think about the products and packaging they consume. Look at the effects various items have on the environment.
- Pot and package the following plants. They act as natural air cleaners, filtering common indoor air pollutants such as formaldehyde, benzene and tricholorethylene. Look for aloe plant (aloe vera), spider plant, pot mum, golden pothos, peace lily and English ivy. This task could be incorporated into a study of plants, gardening, the environment or pollution.
- These "gifts to the earth" can be made as gifts for various occasions or can be sold at a school fund-raising event.

Chapter 2

Bubble Brews

Bubbles, amazing bubbles. Easy to make. A wonder to watch. They float and swirl and disappear or burst before your eyes.

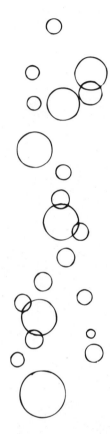

- Good Bubble Weather–The best bubbles are made on cool days, with high humidity and no wind. Bubbles last longer when there is water in the air. Early evenings, night and early mornings are usually good times for bubbling.

- The best surface for bubble making is a paved, nonslip surface–like a school yard. A group of children and their bubble brews might be more suds than the school lawn can handle.

- Bend thin coat hangers or pipe cleaners into loops for bubble blowers.

- To make enormous bubbles, dip the large end of a plastic kitchen funnel into the solution and blow through the small end.

- Joy™ or Dawn™ commercial dish soaps work best for bubbles.

- The longer your solution sits, the better it gets.

- Experiment with common objects as bubble blowers. How about a straw or a key ring? Have students bring in as many potential bubble-blowing devices as they can find.

Small Blower

K-3

Materials:

thin wire
scissors or wire cutter
duct tape

Process:

1. Cut wire about 5" to 7" (12.7 to 17.78 cm) long.

2. Bend the wire to make a loop.

3. Twist the end of the wire around the handle and tape.

4. Pour bubble brew into a small container about 3" (7.62 cm) deep.

5. Dip the loop into your brew and blow gently on the film in the hole or wave it through the air.

Try This:

• Bend your loop into different shapes.

Hoop Blower

 K-3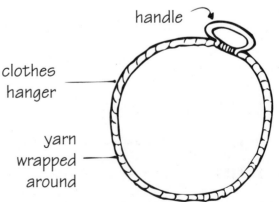

....

Materials:

wire clothes hanger
pliers
duct tape
3 feet (.91 m) of yarn

....

Process:

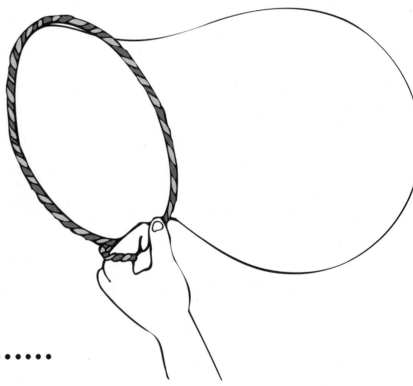

1. Bend the wire hanger into a circle. Use pliers to add an extra twist or two to make the hoop smaller.

2. Wrap the hoop with tape so it is safe–this will be your handle.

3. Wrap yarn around the hoop. The yarn will soak up the soap and grip the soap film.

4. Dip the hoop and pull it out.

....

Try This:

• Try to catch a small bubble inside a large one. Form the large bubble around the small one.

handle

clothes hanger

yarn wrapped around

Bubble Brew

K-3

Materials:

1 quart (.95 l) water
2-quart (1.9 l) bottle with a
    tight lid
4 ounces (118.28 ml) liquid
    dishwashing soap or
    detergent
measuring cup
3 T (45 ml) glycerine (avail-
    able at drugstores)
bowl

Process:

1. Put the water into the bottle.

2. Add dishwashing soap.

3. Add the glycerine.

4. Put the lid on the bottle and shake it up.

5. Let the mixture sit in a warm place for about 30 minutes.

Try This:

- If you see froth in the solution, clear it away with a dry finger, or it will interfere with the film needed for large soap bubbles.
- Make the Best Brew Center. Have students stir up their own brews to find the right combination of ingredients. This will take a lot of group interaction, experimentation, recording and problem solving.

Super Giant Bubbles

K-3

Bubbles beyond belief!

Materials:

³/₄ cup (180 ml) cold clear water
1 T (15 ml) sugar
¹/₄ cup (60 ml) clear liquid dish soap
¹/₄ cup (60 ml) glycerine (available at drugstores)
large flat dish or pan
bubble hoop

Process:

1. Stir water and sugar together.

2. Add glycerine and soap.

3. Let sit for 20 minutes.

4. Stir well and pour into a large flat container for making your bubbles.

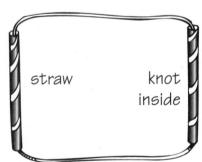

straw   knot inside

Try This:

- Add more glycerine to make the bubbles even stronger.
- Dip the hoop into the solution then wave it in the air.
- Try using a straw-and-yarn bubble maker. Thread a 2¹/₂ foot (.76 m) length of string through two straws. Tie the ends together. Dip your straw-and-yarn bubble maker into the solution. Lift out by the straws.
- Make a soap film floor to bounce other bubbles on or wave it through the air and flip your wrist a little to set the bubble free. Is your bubble square? Can you trap a smaller bubble inside as you wave and flip?

18

Frozen Bubbles

K-3

A cool activity with great results.

Materials: bubble solution   bubble blower   cold weather

Process:

1. Blow some bubbles on a calm wintry day when the temperature is below 32°F (0°C). On a very cold day bubbles freeze almost instantly.

2. Blow your bubble inside, catch it and take it out. The bubble will freeze. Watch the frozen spot grow until the bubble breaks because it has lost its elasticity.

3. Watch the frozen section float off into the winter day.

Try This:

- Try poking a hole in the bubble before it breaks. If you are really tricky, you might be able to blow a smaller bubble into the hole!
- Some people have reported blowing bubbles that don't break when they freeze. Try your hand at it.

Bubbly Soda

K-3

Tiny bubbles that will amaze you.

Materials:
small jar
4 ounces (118.28 ml) soda pop
1 tsp of salt

Process:
1. Fill a small baby food jar half full of soda pop.

2. Add salt.

3. Observe as bubbles form and then rise to the top.

Try This:
• Introduce the scientific method of investigation. Have students write up this simple experiment.
• Add a peanut to the jar.

Bubble Art

Materials:

paint shirts
tablecloth
flat pan
1 cup (250 ml) water
3 T (45 ml) liquid tempera paint
1 T (15 ml) dishwashing detergent
straws
paper

Process:

1. Cover children's clothing with paint shirts and cover the work surface with a plastic tablecloth.

2. Pour the water, paint and detergent into bowl or pan.

3. Children will bring their straws to the mixture, put one end in and blow. Practice blowing before the straw goes in. Ensure children know the difference between blowing out and sucking in!

4. Blow and blow until the bubbles are bubbling out of the container.

5. Gently place the paper over the top of the bowl, allowing the paper to touch the bubbles.

6. Remove the paper and allow it to dry. "Bubble up" for the next paper.

Try This:

- Provide groups with the ingredients to make their own bowl of bubbles–each in a different color. Allow experimentation with varying amounts of paint. Children can rotate from group to group creating colorful bubble pictures.
- When the papers have dried, cut them into the shape of bubbles for a bubbly display. Students can write bubble poems on these bubbles.
- Shape the bubble art into fans for a wonderful effect.

* Caution: Blow through the straw!

Purple Volcano

K-3

Tiny bubbles with a colorful twist!

Materials:

1 tall, skinny glass
4 ounces (118.28 ml) purple grape juice (must be real grape juice)
4 tsp (20 ml) baking soda
4 tsp (20 ml) white vinegar

Process:

1. Fill the glass half full with grape juice.

2. Stir in a small spoonful of baking soda.

3. Watch for amazing results.

4. Now add 1 teaspoon (5 ml) of white vinegar and look for the foam and color change again. Continue alternating vinegar and soda for bubbly, colorful fun.

Try This:

- The carbon dioxide bubbles are by-products of the combination of vinegar and baking soda. The grape juice helps us see those bubbles.
- Set up a science table where students can experiment with various combinations. With a little soap, vinegar, water, baking soda, food coloring and soda pop, you will set the stage for safe bubbly fun.

Bubble Up

K-3

Materials:

glass
2 ounces (59.14 ml) white vinegar
3 seashells

Process:

1. Pour vinegar into a glass.

2. Add the seashells.

3. If there is limestone in the shells, you'll have your very own bubble factory!

Try This:

- Bubble Center: Provide students with a vinegar bath and an assortment of items. Have students predict which ones will produce bubbles when set in the bath. Can students explain why some do and some don't?

Bubble Power

K-3

Materials:

1 tsp (5 ml) active dry yeast
1/4 cup (60 ml) sugar
1 cup (250 ml) warm water
1 small balloon with a neck that will stretch over the top of the bottle
1 quart (.95 l) soda pop bottle
funnel
bowl

Process:

1. Blow the balloon up and then let the air out to "stretch" it.

2. Combine the sugar, the yeast and the water in the bottle. You might need the funnel.

3. Hold your hand over the bottle opening and shake to mix it all up.

4. Fit the balloon over the opening in the bottle.

5. Set the bottle into a bowl filled with almost-hot water.

6. Let it sit for about 1 hour.

7. Observe.

Try This:

- Before the task, ask students what will happen. Record their guesses.
- After the project, ask students why they think this happened.
- The yeast fed on the sugar and produced carbon dioxide which filled the balloon. Have students look for little holes in a loaf of bread or a cake.
- Try this with 1/4 cup (60 ml) vinegar in the bottle and 2 T (30 ml) of baking soda in the balloon–no bowl of warm water needed. When the balloon is fitted on the bottle and the soda meets the vinegar, carbon dioxide is released and the balloon fills up.
- Discuss other forms of gases.

24

Chapter 3

Crystal Creations
Rainbow Crystal Garden

2-3   1

Fascinating!

Materials:

2 charcoal briquettes
6 T (90 ml) iodized salt
1 T (15 ml) household ammonia
6 T (90 ml) laundry bluing

6 T (90 ml) water
throwaway aluminum pie tin
food coloring
container

Process:

1. In a container, mix together 1 or 2 tablespoons (15 or 30 ml) each of liquid bluing, iodized salt and ammonia and water.

2. Stir to dissolve as much salt as possible.

3. Break the charcoal into chunks and place into the disposable pie tin.

4. Add a few drops of food coloring to each piece.

5. Pour the liquid solution over top of charcoal pieces.

6. Within an hour, frosty formations will begin to appear and will continue to grow almost indefinitely.

7. Add more liquid solution as it evaporates.

8. Admire the beautiful colors and shapes carefully. The crystal formations are so fragile that even a little bump of the table will cause them to crumble.

Try This:

- For the sake of safety, do this activity ahead of time and let your class see the results.
- Give students materials to sketch the crystal formations they see.
- Give students various colors of paint to try to re-create the beautiful colors.

* Caution: Be careful when handling ammonia. Use materials in a well-ventilated area.

Crystal and Needles

Materials:

4 T (60 ml) Epsom salts
1 cup (250 ml) water
measuring cup
black construction paper
scissors
lid from a large jar

Process:

1. Cut a circle from black paper that will fit inside the lid.

2. Place the paper in the lid.

3. Add 4 tablespoons (60 ml) Epsom salts to the water in the measuring cup and stir until clear.

4. Pour a very thin layer of the mixture into the lid.

5. Let stand undisturbed for 24 hours.

Long needle-shaped crystals will form on the black paper as the water evaporates.

Try This:

- Find out why the crystals formed. Ask students to speculate.
- When the water evaporated, it left the salts which arranged themselves into a crystal pattern. Sugar, salt and other substances form their own particular type of pattern. Have students compare the patterns from the various projects.
- Lead a "crystal hike." Students take pencil and paper and record things that look like crystal patterns around the school and school yard.
- Many art activities can arise from the study of crystal formations. Have students create their own patterns with various artistic media.

Salty Crystals

K-3

Materials:

1/2 cup (125 ml) water
1/4 cup (60 ml) salt
bowl
spoon

Process:

1. Stir the water and salt together in a bowl.

2. Allow the bowl to sit undisturbed in a warm place until all the water evaporates (3 to 4 weeks).

3. Slow evaporation of the water leaves behind clear cubic salt crystals called halite.

Try This:

- Put one bowl of this solution in a cool place and one in a warm place. What differences are observed? Are there any theories to explain the differences?
- Look at the crystals through a magnifying glass.

Candy on a String

Recovering solute crystals–an experiment you can eat.

Materials:

1/2 cup (125 ml) water
1 cup (250 ml) granulated sugar
wooden spoon
measuring cup
small saucepan
small shallow dishes
stove
string
craft stick

Process:

1. Stir water and a spoonful of sugar in the pan over low heat.

2. Add spoonfuls of sugar, one at a time, stirring each addition until it dissolves.

3. Continue heating gently until all sugar is dissolved.

4. Boil for 1 minute until the solution is thick and clear with no crystals.

5. Pour hot solution into dishes.

6. Let stand.

7. Tie one end of the string to a craft stick.

8. Lay a string in the center of the dish. The sugar crystals will form on it.

Try This:

- Observe the crystalization process with a magnifying glass.
- Look at sugar with a magnifying glass and then with a microscope.
- Encourage students to observe and discuss what they see happening.

28

Gruesome Goodies

Everyone loves to hate the sight and feel of creepy things. Offer disgusting, educational fun to teach *and delight* students.

- Haunted tales add extra pizzazz to these gruesome goodies! Try some creative (not too scary) storytelling.

Slime

K-3

A gross' em out recipe.

Materials:

1 cup (250 ml) cornstarch
1 cup (250 ml) water (You might not need it all.)
green food coloring

square pan or basin
spoon
plastic table cover

Process:

1. Add food coloring to water.

2. Pour ½ cup (125 ml) of cornstarch into a bowl.

3. Add water, a few drops at a time and stir.

4. Continue adding water and cornstarch until the mixture seems to become a thick liquid.

5. Use your hands to combine the ingredients when it gets tough to stir.

6. Explore this stuff!

7. When you are through with your slime, let it dry in the pan overnight and then scrape into the garbage.

Try This:

• Pat the mixture with the palm of your hand. Slap it. Try to pick it up. Hold it; pat it; stroke it. Is it wet or dry? Is it a solid or a liquid? It seems like a solid, but it feels slimy!
• Lead a discussion: Is it a liquid or a solid? Discuss properties of both.
• Use this concoction to stimulate language development. Encourage kids to talk about how it feels, how they feel touching it and what it reminds them of. Make a list of adjectives to describe it. Have students write a story about it.
• The grains of starch are packed together but spaced evenly apart. Slow movement allows the grains to keep their spacing and slide past one another like a liquid. Quick movement or pressure jams the grains together making it act like a solid.
• The slime teaches us a lesson in patience. If you approach life with thought and patience, you will get through anything–if you barge through without thinking, you may have a harder time and end up in a mess! Challenge students to tell or write a fable based on this mixture.

Mold Garden

K-3

What better garden could there be for Halloween?

Materials:

1 slice of white bread with no preservatives
paper napkin
small dish
water
clear plastic bag with ventilation holes

Process:

1. Soak the napkin and place it on the dish.

2. Put the bread on the napkin in the dish.

3. Moisten the bread with a few drops of water.

4. Slip the bread into the plastic bag.

5. Let it sit in a dark place for four or more days.

Try This:

- Look at the bread every day. Record any findings.
- Look at the bread with a microscope or magnifying glass. You should be able to see groups of tiny microscopic organisms called molds. Although these molds are in the air and on surfaces all round us, we only see them when they grow in great numbers as they do in the environment created on the bread.

Recipe for a Haunted House

1-3

Materials:

blindfolds
unbreakable containers
cooked spaghetti
peeled grapes
peanut butter
frozen gelatin
slime (See page 30.)
soapy water
plastic bugs
gauze strips
chestnuts in pods
wintergreen LifeSavers™

Process:

1. Invite students to your haunted house.

2. Blindfold each one and have them feel the contents of the bowls as you explain what each article is.

3. Set up bowls with the following items in them. For some gruesome fun, suggest what each item could be.

cooked spaghetti	brains
peeled grapes	eyes
slime	bats' blood
frozen gelatin	poison ooze
soapy water with plastic bugs	goblin's stew
gauze strips	spider's web
chestnuts in pods	fighting spiders
wintergreen LifeSavers™	ghostly glowing candy (crunch one in the dark and see!)
peanut butter	rotting matter

Recipe for a Haunted House

Try This:
- Encourage kids to create their own haunted house in the classroom. Allow students to think up the ghoulish goodies and offer them to the class.
- Incorporate with a discussion of the senses and of textures.

Creepy Clay

K-3

Materials:

½ cup (125 ml) white glue
1½ cups (375 ml) distilled water
1 tsp (5 ml) borax powder

food coloring
2 small bowls
spoon

Process:

1. Stir glue and ½ cup (125 ml) water in the small bowl.

2. Add drops of coloring until you get just the right shade–green is gruesome.

3. In the other bowl combine borax with 1 cup (250 ml) of water.

4. Stir until the borax is completely dissolved.

5. Stir the borax mixture constantly while adding the glue mixture a little at a time.

6. Carefully dump the blob of clay onto a flat surface.

7. Knead until smooth and pliable.

8. Squeeze it; bounce it; stretch it; sculpt it. Explore!

9. Store in a covered container for up to one week.

Try This:

• Ask students to describe the feel of this rubbery clay. Use a flip chart to record their adjectives.

* Caution: Be careful using borax powder.

Rubber Egg

K-3

Kids will love to hate the look and feel of this egg!

Materials:

egg
wide-mouthed jar
white vinegar

Process:

1. Place the egg in the jar and fill it three-fourths full of vinegar.

2. Leave it for three days.

3. Take it out of the vinegar and discover a new sensation. The egg will have lost its hard shell and have only a membrane. It is quite durable in this form, but use a drop cloth or observe and feel it outdoors!

Try This:

• Encourage students to touch and describe this egg.

Bendy Bones

K-3

. . . .

Materials:

chicken or turkey bones
1 quart (1 liter) of vinegar
large jar

. . . .

Process:

1. Clean bones thoroughly. (They can be boiled or scrubbed.)

2. Dry the bones for two days.

3. Put the bones into a jar and cover them with vinegar. This removes the calcium from the bones.

4. Let stand until the bones are bendable–about seven days–depending on the size of the bone.

5. Remove the bones. They won't rattle, but they will bend!

. . . .

Try This:

- Incorporate with a study of the skeletal system. Minerals make our bones strong and hard. The vinegar removes the minerals from the bone in this experiment.
- Use these bendy bones for some Halloween fun.
- Boil the bones from an entire chicken or turkey and glue them onto thick paper in creative skeletal formations for a dinosaur or Halloween unit.

36

Chapter 5

Critter Treats

We all love to watch the critters. Set out these treats and sit back and enjoy the wildlife.

● ●

- You can make bird feeders from plastic containers, plastic bottles, old milk cartons and if you are ambitious–wood. Hang your feeder in a sheltered place safe from climbing cats or squirrels.

- If you put out a feeder, birds will come to count on that food for their winter survival.

- Fill your feeder right after a snowstorm when the birds will need the food most.

Food Preferences
of Common Birds

• •

small to medium seeds: sparrows, mourning doves, meadowlarks, orioles, red-winged blackbirds

large seeds: cardinals, blue jays

black oil sunflower seed: cardinals, chickadees, titmice, grosbeaks, finches, downy woodpeckers, orioles

striped sunflower: titmice, cardinals, jays, grosbeaks

millet: doves and sparrows

niger thistle: finches

hulled sunflower: finches, jays, cardinals, chickadees

safflower: cardinals, doves, sparrows

corn: sparrows, jays, doves, downy woodpeckers

fruit: catbirds, orioles, redwings, robins, tanagers

large berries (holly, juniper):   cardinals, blue jays, robins

earthworms: robins

crawling insects: towhees, killdeer, robins, nuthatches

flying insects: swallows, house wrens, bluebirds, meadowlarks, red-winged blackbirds

suet: white-breasted nuthatches, black-capped chickadees

nectar: hummingbirds, orioles

Bird Bread

K-3

Materials:

stale bread, doughnuts or
  unsalted pretzels
cookie cutters, knife or
  scissors
peanut butter or lard
tray
yarn or string
birdseed

Process:

1. Cut bread with cookie cutters, or use doughnuts or pretzels. Let them go stale.

2. Spread bread, doughnuts or pretzel with peanut butter then press into a tray of birdseed.

3. Hang the edible ornaments from a tree with yarn or string. Take care not to use nylon or plastic as birds may use these for nesting materials.

Try This:

- Hang a diary, a pair of binoculars and a bird identification book or chart by the window. Bird-watchers record their sightings. Record things like the exact spot the bird is seen, what it is doing, how big it is, what shape it is, its color and markings and if a call is heard.
- Birds are generally looking for food or a mate. Students can record in their Bird-Watching Diary what they think the bird is doing.

Scoop and Fill Bird Stations

K-3

Materials:
half of an orange or grapefruit
suet
birdseed

Process:

1. Scoop out an orange or grapefruit.

2. Fill it halfway with suet and birdseed and place in crook of a tree branch where you can observe the birds.

Try This:

• Variation: Saw coconut shells in half, drill holes and have students thread string through holes to make this shell feeder hang. Fill with seed and other goodies.

Bird Strings

K-3

Materials:
edible berries (cranberries, strawberries, blueberries)
peanuts in their shells
apple slices
popped corn
heavy cotton thread
needle
heavy string

Process:

1. Double the thread and thread the needle.

2. String any variation of berries, apple slices, peanuts and popcorn.

3. Hang this string feeder on a tree where you can watch the birds and enjoy.

Try This:

- Use the school Christmas tree for a bird feeder and bird shelter. Stand it in a snowbank and hang your bird feeder on it. It makes a lovely Christmas gift to the birds. Do this the day before Christmas break.

Bird Cones

K-3

Materials:

string or yarn
large pinecones
peanut butter or suet
birdseed

Process:

1. Tie a string or piece of bright yarn to a large pinecone.

2. Spread the pinecone with peanut butter and roll it in birdseed.

3. Hang it on a tree outside the classroom window or let students take home to hang.

Try This:

- Have plastic bags handy if students will be taking this project home.
- Hang these cones, along with other bird foods, in the discarded Christmas tree.
- Incorporate this with a theme on nutrition. All living things need the right foods to survive and keep healthy.

Hummer Food

It's for the *humming*birds!

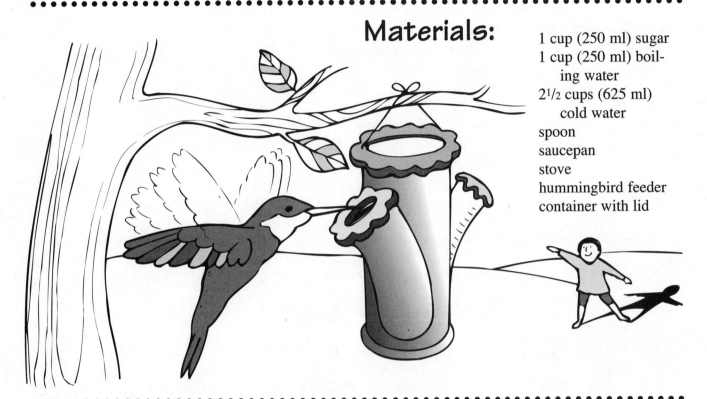

Materials:

1 cup (250 ml) sugar
1 cup (250 ml) boil-
   ing water
2$\frac{1}{2}$ cups (625 ml)
   cold water
spoon
saucepan
stove
hummingbird feeder
container with lid

Process:

1. Boil water in saucepan.

2. Add sugar to the boiling water and stir until the mixture is clear.

3. Add 2$\frac{1}{2}$ cups (625 ml) of cold water.

4. Pour into bird feeder and refrigerate remaining food in the container with lid.

Try This:

• Hang the feeder outside your classroom window.
• Provide research materials so students can find out all sorts of interesting trivia about this little bird. They will be interested to know that the hummingbird's nest would fit in their palm. They eat flower nectar, small insects and spiders. They are very aggressive. They will fight bumble-bees. They can fly, hover in mid-air, speed forward and stop with amazing accuracy and speed.

* Caution: Be careful with hot liquid!

Rover's Snack

K-3

For the dog in your life.

• •

Materials:

water	large bowl
1/4 cup (60 ml) beef broth	spoon
1 package active dry yeast	cutting board
1 tsp (5 ml) sugar	knife
1 1/2 cups (375 ml) tomato juice	rolling pin
1 cup (250 ml) all-purpose flour	spatula
1 1/2 cups (375 ml) wheat germ	cookie sheet
2 1/2 cups (625 ml) whole wheat flour	stove

• •

Process:

1. Preheat oven to 300°F (154°C).

2. Stir water and broth in bowl.

3. Add yeast and let stand for 5 minutes.

4. Add tomato juice, 1 cup (250 ml) all-purpose flour and wheat germ.

5. Stir with a large spoon until mixture forms a batter.

6. Add the remaining all-purpose and whole wheat flours.

7. Dig in and stir with your hands.

8. Form dough into small balls and place on floured cutting board.

9. Roll the balls with the rolling pin to about 1/4" (.6 cm) thick.

10. Use a sharp knife to cut the flattened dough into dog bone shapes.

11. Use a spatula to put your bones on a cookie sheet.

12. Bake at 300°F (154°C) for one hour, turn oven off and leave bones in oven for 4 hours.

Rover's Snack

K-3

Try This:

- Make this a "gift" for Christmas or a special day devoted to animals–for your pet, a grandparent's or a friend's.
- Integrate with a unit on pets.
- Write the recipe on chart paper. Assign each task to a student or group of students.
- Incorporate math measuring and time lessons with this recipe. Assign students to measure and time the activity.

Squirrel Cobs

1-3

A simple treat to make for the furry critters.

Materials:

string
cobs of corn (1 per child)

Process:

1. Husk the corn, leaving a 1" (2.54 cm) piece of stalk at the end of the cob.

2. Tie string firmly around the end of the stalk so the corn will hang. This may take several knots and rounds of string.

3. Hang the corn from a tree or other overhanging area where the squirrels can feast and you can watch!

Try This:

- Incorporate this activity with a study of squirrels or corn.
- Discuss various locations for hanging the cob of corn. Why might some locations be more desirable than others?
- Hang the cobs out for the squirrels for a special holiday–Thanksgiving or Christmas perhaps.
- Plant the corn with your class in the spring and "harvest" it with your new class in the fall. (You might like to share it with your previous student's classes.)
- Smooth the earth beneath the hanging cob and go back later to study squirrel tracks.
- Do not use plastic or wire in place of the string (even if the squirrels bite through the string and run off with the corn!); it would be harmful to other animals.

Chapter 6

Catch a Scent
Petrified Orange

1-3

Materials:

For each student:
½ cup (125 ml) cloves
small thin-skinned orange

paper bag
ribbon

Process:

1. Stick cloves in orange in an interesting pattern that covers almost the entire surface of the orange.

2. Place in a paper bag in a cool place until the fruit has dried out–about three weeks.

3. Remove, add a bright ribbon and hang your petrified orange pomander. The spicy smell will last for years.

Try This:

- Make this for a gift for a special day like Mother's Day, Grandparents' Day or Christmas.
- Set up a Center for the Senses where students can smell various spices and substances. Use blindfolds and play a guessing game with strong scented items.

Potpourri Satchels

K-3

Materials:

herbs or spices (cinnamon, ginger, cloves or anise)
dried flowers (find flowers with a scent)
8" (20.32 cm) square pieces of cheesecloth, netting or muslin
ribbon or string
grinding stone
scissors

Process:

1. Separate flower petals.

2. Crush herbs or spices with fingers or on a grinding stone.

3. Place flowers and spices into the center of the material.

4. Tie securely with ribbon or string.

5. Use a satchel in your drawer or give as a gift.

Try This:

- Take students on a hike to search for materials for this activity. You might make use of a plant and wildflower identification guide.
- Dry your own herbs, spices or flowers by hanging them upside down in a dry place.

48

Homemade Perfume

K-3

Materials:

grinding stone
selection of lemons, limes,
    apples, herbs, mint leaves,
    rose petals, lavender leaves
blossoms of scented flowers
water or grain alcohol
sieve
small glass containers with
    tight-fitting lids
bottle

Process:

1. Break the scent material with your fingers and then on grinding stone.

2. Place this material into the bottle.

3. Fill to the top with grain alcohol (or water).

4. Let sit for two weeks. If it does not smell like the material, add more material and let sit a bit longer.

5. Pour clear liquid through sieve into fancy containers.

6. Seal the bottle with a cap or cork.

Try This:

- Decorate a baby food jar or fancy bottle and give perfume as a gift to someone special.
- Experiment with mixing foods, herbs and flowers to invent your own unique scents.
- Variation: When using water in place of grain alcohol, let sit for only one day. Use within a few days.

* Caution: Be careful using grain alcohol!

Soapy Sculptures

K-3   ✿

Materials:

2 cups (480 ml) Ivory Snow™ detergent
4 T (60 ml) water
food coloring
bowl

Process:

1. Pour detergent in bowl.

2. Mix water and food coloring to desired shade.

3. Using your hands, gradually work colored water into soap until it forms a clay of sorts.

4. Add more water if the mixture is too dry or more soap if it is too wet to work.

5. Sculpt into interesting shapes.

6. This soap can be used at school on messy little hands or given on special days as a welcome, practical gift.

Try This:

- Young children can shape snowballs and snowmen with this soap.
- Let students experiment with colors.
- Make soap eggs and put them in an egg carton.
- Incorporate this activity with a unit on pioneers and their soap-making techniques.

50

Creations to Burn

A neat way to use old crayon stubs and create something wonderful to light up the dark!

• Candles are easy to make but call for safety precautions. These wax wonders are too good to pass up–so invite volunteers, stress the importance of caution around wax and proceed. Use your judgement and allow students to participate only where you feel it is appropriate for your particular group.

Homemade Candles

2-3

Materials:

cans or sturdy cardboard containers such as
    milk cartons
crayon or candle stubs, paraffin or beeswax
    (1 lb [.45 kg] for four 2" [5.08 cm] can-
    dles)
large tin can
saucepan
candle wicking (available at craft supply
    stores)
small stick (craft stick or pencil)
tape
stove

Process:

1. Peel wrappers from used crayons and break into small pieces. Drop into old pan or coffee can, set in a pan of warm water on the stove.

2. Heat at medium heat until the wax is melted.

3. Pour the warm wax into the container.

4. Tape one end of the wick to a stick, hang the wick in the center of the candle resting the stick on the sides of the container.

5. Let the candle harden for 8 hours.

6. Peel away the conatiner.

7. Trim the wick.

Try This:

- For striped candles, let layers of different colors harden before pouring in the next layer.
- Wicks can be predipped in a hard wax available from dental office suppliers, or wicks can be hung over can with a weighted end to keep the wick taut.
- Pour wax into blown out eggs with one open end.

* Caution: Be careful when heating and handling wax!

52

Sand Candles

1-3

....

Materials:

large basin full of sand, sand table or sand pit
crayons, candle stubs, beeswax or paraffin wax
    (1 lb [.45 kg] makes three or four 2" [5.08 cm] candles)
tin
double boiler
water
pot holders
small stone
small stick (craft stick or pencil)
candle wicking (available at craft supply stores)
trowel

....

Process:

1. Dig a hole in the sand about 4" (10.16 cm) wide and 8" (20.32 cm) deep.

2. Peel papers off crayon stubs. Break crayons into small bits and put in a tin.

3. Attach one end of the wick to the stick and the other to a stone.

4. Fill the pot halfway with hot water.

5. Put the tin of wax in the water and warm at low heat until the wax has melted. As the wax melts you can add more pieces and stir.

6. Carefully carry the tin of wax to the hole in the sand and pour in the wax.

7. Lower the wick into the middle of the wax. The stone will weigh it down, and the stick will hold the wick straight.

8. Allow the wax to cool and harden completely. This will take about 6 hours.

9. Use a trowel to ease the sand away from the candle. Lift the candle out.

10. Brush off excess, trim the wick and admire.

* Caution: Be careful when heating and handling wax!

Sand Candles

Try This:

- Children dig the sand holes and dig their candles out but observe the wax melting and pouring.
- Students can place interesting objects around the edges of the sand hole. These will become part of the candle when the wax hardens.

Have child dig a hole in the sand.

HOT WAX!

SAND

Finished Candle Dug Out of Sand

* Caution: Be careful when heating and handling wax!

54

Snow Candles

Materials:
crayon stubs, candle stubs or
    paraffin wax
container: milk carton, glass or
    plastic container
prewaxed candle wick

small stick (craft stick or pencil)
small stone
tape
pot
tin can

Process:

1. Put wax in the tin can.

2. Heat water in a pot.

3. Put the tin of wax in the pot and melt the wax.

4. When the wax is thoroughly melted, take the tin outside.

5. Dig a hole in the snow where wax will be poured.

6. Tie or tape one of the prewaxed wick ends to the stick. Attach the other end to the stone.

7. Pour the wax into the snow.

8. Hang the wick into the wax with the stone weighing the wick down and the stick resting across the top of the snow.

9. As the ice and snow melt, the edges will harden and your candle will take on a delicate design.

10. Let the candle harden thoroughly before moving–about 3 hours.

Try This:

- Have students dig the "snow mold" for the wax that will be poured by an adult.
- Variation: Bring snow into the classroom and pack around edges of containers. The wax will be poured into the individual snow-packed containers.

* Caution: Be careful when heating and handling wax!

Chapter 8

Neat to Eat
Rubber Dessert Eggs

1-3   over 1 hour O.K.

Colorful eggs you can eat. Makes 6 large eggs.

• •

Materials:

2 envelopes unflavored gelatin
1 package (3 ounces [88.71 kg])
   fruit-flavored gelatin
1 1/2 cups (375 ml) boiling water
prepared eggshells

large needle
bowls
measuring cup
funnel

• •

Process:

1. Wash eggs and with a large needle, pierce the narrow end of the egg breaking the membrane and yolk. Make a hole about 1/2" (1.25 cm) wide.

2. Hold egg over small bowl and shake the contents out.

3. Rinse the inside of the egg well and let dry thoroughly (narrow end up) in egg carton.

4. In a medium bowl, combine unflavored gelatin and flavored gelatin.

5. Add boiling water and stir until gelatin is completely dissolved.

6. Cool 10 minutes.

7. Using a measuring cup and funnel, pour mixture into hole in eggshells.

8. Chill until firm–about 2 hours.

9. Peel the outer shell of the egg and then the membrane to reveal the shimmery, jewel-like egg you can eat. The eggs will stay firm, smooth and shiny at room temperature.

• •

Try This:

• Serve at Easter or for a spring unit.
• Incorporate this activity with a study of eggs.
• Make a nest of lettuce leaves to serve these.
• Discuss how the eggs feel and look.
• Play a game of Pass the Egg–every student has a spoon, and the eggs are passed from spoon to spoon. Make it a cooperative effort that builds group and fine motor skills.

Apple Leather

K-3   O.K.

A fun, healthy chew!

Materials:

6 firm apples
apple peeler
knife
string
darning needle
paper bag

Process:

1. Peel the apples.

2. Cut out the cores.

3. Slice apples into pieces about 1/2" (1.25 cm) thick.

4. Put about a yard of string through the eye of a darning needle.

5. Thread the apple pieces onto the string like beads. Don't let the apple pieces touch one another. Use extra strings if you need them.

6. Hang up the strings like a food clothesline.

7. Turn the apples every other day.

8. Remove the leather apple rings on the seventh day, and eat them or store them in a paper bag for later.

Try this:

- Integrate this activity with a study of harvest.
- Talk about nutrition.
- Observe the changes on a daily basis.

Melon Bowl

Materials:

1 large watermelon
1 cantaloupe melon
1 other seasonal melon
berries in season
blunt knives

sharp knife
melon baller
fruit cups
spoons
cutting board

Process:

1. Cut the melon in half.

2. Have children remove the insides of the melon with spoons until only the shell remains. Reserve the insides on the cutting board.

3. Allow children to cut the melon into bite-size pieces using blunt knives. (Melon is very easy to cut!)

4. Children can use the melon baller to get scoops of watermelon, cantaloupe, etc.

5. Put all of the melon pieces into the melon bowl.

6. Add seasonal fruit, toss and serve.

Try This:

- Grow your own melons with the children if the seasons permit in your area.
- Invite children to design their own way of making melon shapes. Do cookie cutters work? What happens when different kinds of spoons are used?
- Save the melon seeds for seed pictures, jewelry or manipulative math activities. (Be prepared for seed spitting contests–use your own discretion!)
- Use this as an end-of-the-year treat.

* Caution: Use very blunt knives!

Yogurt Pops

K-3

Materials:

To make approximately 20 pops:
2 cups (500 ml) plain yogurt
1¼ cups (310 ml) frozen concentrated orange juice
1 tsp (5 ml) vanilla
bowl
spoon
ice cube trays
craft sticks

Process:

1. Place the yogurt, frozen juice and vanilla in the bowl.

2. Stir hard until everything is mixed together.

3. Scrape the mixture into ice cube trays.

4. Place a wooden craft stick in each cube.

5. Put the trays into the freezer and leave at least 4 hours.

Try This:

- For different flavors, use frozen grape or pineapple juice instead of orange juice.
- Talk about nutritious treats. Make a chart. Help students to recognize what is good for their bodies.

Ice Berries

K-3

Materials:

berries (in season)
cookie sheet
colander
drying cloth
freezer

Process:

1. Pick or purchase fresh berries.

2. Wash berries in a colander.

3. Allow berries to drain and dry thoroughly. Gentle drying with a towel will speed this process along.

4. On a cookie sheet, space the berries so they are not touching, and place them in the freezer until frozen, about 30 to 60 minutes depending upon the berry size.

5. Remove berries from freezer and add to drinks to chill as you would with ice cubes.

Try This:

• Freeze smaller berries in clumps. Try shaping these into creatures.
• Drop small berries in ice cube trays, add water and freeze. The fruit will appear to "float" inside of the ice cube.
• Incorporate this activity into a study of changes in the state of matter, temperature or weather.
• Have students experiment with the length of time it takes different berries to freeze and thaw. Does size make a difference? Why or why not? Does a wrapped berry freeze and thaw at a different rate?
• Try freezing other fruits–lemons, oranges, cherries, peaches and melon. How do they change? Discuss methods of preserving foods used in the past and the present.

* Caution: Small berries can be a choking hazard!

Ice Arrangements

K-3

Materials:

container (small plastic margarine tub or cutoff milk carton)
water
assortment of berries, fruit, mint leaves or edible flower petals
freezer

Process:

1. Fill the container half full with water.

2. Freeze until hard.

3. Brush water on the ice and arrange flowers, fruit, berries or petals on the ice.

4. Freeze until arrangement stays in place–about 30 minutes.

5. Cover arrangement with water and freeze again.

6. Remove from freezer and let thaw until the ice arrangement can be popped from the container. This can be achieved more quickly if the container is set in hot water for 5 minutes.

7. Float the arrangment in a punch bowl or lemonade pitcher.

Try This:

- Have each child make an ice arrangement or "ice pie" and display outside on a cold day–or for a short time on a hot day.
- Freeze a wooden stick frame inside a square pan. Create a picture inside the frame using various visually interesting items. Cover with water and freeze again. Remove from the pan and admire the framed ice masterpiece. String can be looped and frozen in the back of the picture so that the artwork can be hung outside in the winter.

Green Things

K-3

Sprout some seeds and eat 'em up.

Materials:

2 T (30 ml) of untreated seeds–alfalfa, mung (bean sprouts), soybeans, fenu-greek, radishes, peas, sesame, wheat, corn–available at health food, organic or Asian food stores. Most garden seeds are chemically treat-ed–use only those that state otherwise.

cold water
sprouting container (margarine tub, ice-cream container, etc.)
mesh netting
elastic band

Process:

1. Put the seeds in the sprouting container and cover with cold water.

2. Cover with the mesh netting. Hold in place with the elastic band.

3. Soak overnight.

4. In the morning turn the sprouting container upside down over a bowl to drain the seeds.

5. Rinse the sprouts with fresh water two to three times each day. Keep them drained but moist.

6. When the seeds sprout tails–usually between two and five days–they are ready to be eaten. When they taste best to you, put them in the refrigera-tor to stop their growth.

Try This:

• Eat the sprouts raw or cooked. Make sandwiches, salads, stir fry or a soup for a class lunch or snack.
• Have the children experiment and record. Do the beans sprout faster in warmth or cold?
• What differences are noted when the sprouts are kept in the sun versus darkness?
• Students can role-play at being sprouts. What happens when "sun" shines down or "rain" falls on the seeds?
• This activity will integrate well into a study of plants or growth.

62

Sesame Snacks

 1-3

Good-for-you candy. Sweet and nutritious!

Materials:

½ cup (125 ml) peanut butter
½ cup (125 ml) liquid honey
1 cup (250 ml) skim milk powder
1 cup (250 ml) sesame seeds
2 T (30 ml) chopped nuts

½ cup (125 ml) shredded coconut
saucepan
spoon
cake pan
stove

Process:

1. Measure peanut butter and honey into the saucepan.

2. Place over medium heat.

3. Cook and stir for 3 minutes.

4. Remove the saucepan from the heat.

5. Add the skim milk powder, sesame seeds, coconut and nuts.

6. Stir until everything is well mixed.

7. Press the mixture into the cake pan.

8. Place the pan in the refrigerator until the mixture becomes firm–about 2 hours.

9. Cut into squares.

Try This:

• Enhance a study of seeds with this tasty treat.
• Allow students to taste ingredients individually and then in the end product. Can they distinguish any single taste in the finished recipe?

* Caution: Be careful when using heat source!

Candied Flowers

Materials:

2 egg whites
1/2 cup (125 ml) flower petals
1/2 cup (125 ml) sugar
whisk
wire rack
pastry or clean paintbrush

Process:

1. Gather petals of chemical-free roses or violets–confirm with an identification guide before eating.

2. Gently wash the petals and spread on a wire rack to dry.

3. Whisk the egg whites until frothy.

4. Carefully paint the petals with the egg whites.

5. Sprinkle sugar over the petals and let dry thoroughly until hard.

6. Eat as they are or use to decorate cupcakes or ice cream.

Try This:

• Introduce students to the idea that weeds and wildflowers are valuable sources of food and medicines.
• Use a field guide to help you identify the plants you eat.

* Caution: Remind children that nothing from the wild should be eaten without an adult's verification of its identity!

Curd and Whey

K-3

Great for eating during a nursery rhyme theme.

. . . .

Materials:

1 cup (250 ml) fresh milk
2 T (30 ml) white vinegar
spoon
jar

. . . .

Process:

1. Fill the jar with milk and vinegar.

2. Stir.

3. Let stand for 3 minutes.

4. The milk will separate into the white solid curds and clear liquid whey.

5. Enjoy the curds right away or store in a cool place.

. . . .

Try This:

• Use this activity to enhance a study of nursery rhymes, the dairy farm, pioneers or nutrition.

Butter

K-3

Betty Botter never bought it so good!

Materials:

½ pint (.235 l) heavy cream (whipping cream)
marble
jar with secure lid
salt (optional)
container

Process:

1. Pour cream into jar.

2. Add marble.

3. Put lid on tightly.

4. Shake, shake, shake your way to butter!

5. Pour the buttermilk off and remove the marble.

6. Add a little salt if desired, and put the butter in a container.

7. Eat right away or store in a cool place for later.

Try This:

- Extend a lesson about pioneers with this activity.
- Set up a Tasting Center where students taste various butters and margarines.
- Allow children to experiment with their butter by adding more or less salt, yellow food coloring and a bit of sugar.
- A bread-making activity would go well with this project!
- Ask students to recall and write about the activity.

66

Peanut Butter

 K-3

....

Materials:

peanuts roasted in shells
1 T (15 ml) corn oil
blender
bowl or jar
friends

....

Process:

1. Gather friends to help shell the peanuts.

2. Shell enough peanuts to make 1 cup (250 ml).

3. Rub the red skins off the peanuts.

4. Place the oil in the blender and put on the lid.

5. Turn the blender on.

6. Drop the peanuts a few at a time through the hole in the lid of the blender.

7. Stop blending when the peanut butter is as smooth as you like it.

8. Scrape the peanut butter into a bowl or jar.

9. Eat it right away or store it in a sealed container.

....

Try This:

• Allow children to taste and compare various butters–apple, peanut, dairy.
• What animals eat peanuts? Do they like peanut butter?
• Read and write stories and poems about peanut butter.

Ice Cream

K-3

. . . .

Materials:

1 pint (.47 l) thick cream
1/3 cup (80 ml) sugar or honey
1 tsp (5 ml) vanilla
1 pinch of table salt
aluminum can with a plastic lid

large pot, bowl or pail
wooden spoon with a hole in it
crushed ice cubes, icicles or snow
box of table salt (or rock salt from
   the hardware store)

. . . .

Process:

1. Pour the thick cream into the aluminum can.

2. Add sugar, a pinch of salt and the vanilla and stir well.

3. Poke a hole large enough for the spoon handle in the plastic lid of the aluminum can.

4. Push the spoon handle through the hole and fit the lid onto the can.

5. Fill the base of the pot, bowl or pail with ice. Set the can of the cream mixture on top of the ice.

6. Pour a layer of salt on the ice. Continue layering the ice and salt around the tin until it reaches the top of the tin.

7. Let stand for 5 minutes.

8. Have children take turns twirling the spoon handle to mix the ice cream. Turn the can occasionally.

9. Continue adding layers of ice and salt as the ice melts.

10. After about 15 minutes the spoon will become quite difficult to twirl–this means the ice cream is freezing! Continue twirling until the ice cream has the consistency you desire.

11. When the ice cream has the consistency you desire, remove the can from the ice bucket, remove the spoon from the lid and serve! (If you desire a firmer ice cream, the mixture can be covered and placed in the freezer for about 1 hour.

68

Ice Cream

Try This:

- Experiment with a variety of flavors–berries, fruits, extracts, coffee, chocolate, etc. Stir these in when you are ready to stop twirling or just before you put the mixture in the freezer.
- Read and write stories about ice cream.
- Hand out play money and set up an ice-cream store as part of your math lesson.
- Introduce the concepts of melting and freezing.
- For some added fun, try to eat the ice cream with chopsticks.
- Invent a new ice-cream cone. What else would do the trick?

Bibliography

Atwood, Margaret. Illustrated by John Bianchi. *For the Birds*. Douglas & McIntyre, Toronto, 1990.

Bakule, Paula Dreifus, Ed., *Rodale's Book of Practical Formulas: Easy-to-Make, Easy-to-Use Recipes for Hundreds of Everyday Activities and Tasks*. U.S. Rodale Press, Inc., 1991.

Bell, J.L. Illustrated by Bill Kimber. *Soap Science: A Science Book Bubbling with 36 Experiments*. Kids Can Press, Toronto, 1993. U.S. Distribution: Addison-Wesley.

Better Homes and Gardens. Water Wonders. Meredith Corporation, Des Moines, Iowa. 1989.

Canadian Wildlife Federation/Western Regional Environmental Education Council & the Western Regional Environmental Education Council & the Western Association of Fish and Wildlife Agencies. *Project Wild: Elementary Activity Guide*. Canadian Wildlife Federation, Ottawa, Canada, 1988.

Diehn, Gwen, and Terry Kratwurst. *Nature Crafts for Kids: 50 Fantastic Things to Make with Mother Nature's Help*. Sterling Publishing Co., Inc., New York, 1992.

Erickson, Donna. Illustrated by David LaRochelle. *Prime Time Together . . . with Kids*. Discovery Toys, Augsburg Fortress, Minneapolis, 1989.

Gold, Carol. *The Jumbo Book of Science: 136 of the Best Experiments from the Ontario Science Center*. Kids Can Press, Toronto, 1994. U.S. Distribution: Addison-Wesley.

Graham, Ada. *Foxtails, Ferns and Fish Scales: A Handbook of Art and Nature Projects*. Four Winds Press, 1976.

Gray, Magda. *Rainy Day Pastimes: 215 Ideas to Keep Kids Happy*. Marshall Cavendish, London, 1975.

Griffin, Margaret, and Ruth Griffin. *It's a Gas!* Kids Can Press, Toronto, 1993. U.S. Distribution: IPG Distribution.

Klutz Press Editors. *Everybody's Everywhere Backyard Bird Book*. Klutz Press, Palo Alto, CA, 1992.

Norris, Doreen, and Joyce Boucher. *Observing Children in the Formative Years*. The Board of Education for the city of Toronto, Toronto, 1980.

Wilkes, Angela. *My First Cook Book*. Stoddart Publishing, Toronto, 1989.